AMAZING ANIMALS
Rainforest Romp

D0306533

First published 2009 by Macmillan Children's Books
This edition published 2010 by Macmillan Children's Books
a division of Macmillan Publishers Limited
20 New Wharf Road, London N1 9RR
Basingstoke and Oxford
Associated companies throughout the world
www.panmacmillan.com

ISBN: 978-0-330-53236-5

Text copyright © Tony Mitton 2009
Illustrations copyright © Ant Parker 2009
Moral rights asserted.
Consultancy by David Burnie

All rights reserved. No part of this publication may be reproduced, stored in or introduced
into a retrieval system, or transmitted, in any form, or by any means (electronic, mechanical,
photocopying, recording or otherwise) without the prior written permission of the publisher.
Any person who does any unauthorised act in relation to this publication may be liable
to criminal prosecution and civil claims for damages.

1 3 5 7 9 8 6 4 2

A CIP catalogue record for this book is available from the British Library.

JP

To Jasmine & Freya in Derbyshire - TM
For Geoff and Graham - AP

AMAZING ANIMALS

Rainforest Romp

Tony Mitton and Ant Parker

MACMILLAN CHILDREN'S BOOKS

In South American forests
the trees grow thick and tall.

So many creatures live there,
it's hard to count them all.

The tapir is a mammal.
It's hoofed and rather stout.

It sniffs for tasty plant life
with its clever, stretchy snout.

The giant armadillo has skin
like armoured scales.

Whatever wants to munch it
just hurts its teeth, and fails.

A jaguar's a great big cat that climbs and stalks and swims.

It prowls around for jungle prey
on stealthy, silent limbs.

This snake's an anaconda.
Be careful of it, please.

Don't let it try to cuddle you,
it just might start to squeeze.

Beware the poisonous tree frog.
Although it's cute to see,

its colour is a warning
which tells us, "Let me be!"

These beaky birds are toucans.
They like to live in twos.

For eating fruit and insects
those bills are good to use.

A sloth moves very slowly.
How shy it seems to be.

It likes to live alone,
and hardly ever leaves its tree.

Here are howler monkeys.
They hang around up high.

From far across the forest
you'll hear them as they cry.

Our rainforest romp is over.
Didn't we see a lot!

Toucans, frogs and prowling cats –
but what else did you spot?

Did you spot . . .

the agouti?

the cock-of-the-rock?

the emerald
tree boa?

the silky
anteater?

the spider
monkey?

the golden lion
tamarin?

the uakari
monkey?

the capybara?

the hoatzin?